C000231524

VOLVO LORRIES

BILL REID

AMBERLEY

First published 2017

Amberley Publishing
The Hill, Stroud
Gloucestershire, GL5 4EP

www.amberley-books.com

Copyright © Bill Reid, 2017

The right of Bill Reid to be identified as the Author
of this work has been asserted in accordance with
the Copyrights, Designs and Patents Act 1988.

ISBN 978 1 4456 6772 0 (print)
ISBN 978 1 4456 6773 7 (ebook)

All rights reserved. No part of this book may be
reprinted or reproduced or utilised in any form
or by any electronic, mechanical or other means,
now known or hereafter invented, including
photocopying and recording, or in any information
storage or retrieval system, without the permission
in writing from the Publishers.

British Library Cataloguing in Publication Data.
A catalogue record for this book is available from
the British Library.

Typesetting by Amberley Publishing.
Printed in the UK.

Introduction

Various books have been written chronicling the story of Volvo cars and commercial vehicles. This book records the introduction of Volvo trucks to the UK market and the subsequent growth and success of the marque to the present day.

In 1964, a Volvo L4751 was loaned to a London haulier and ran as a platform lorry. This was a precursor of the Volvo F86, which would make inroads into the UK haulage industry from 1967 when Jim McKelvie set up Ailsa Trucks Ltd in Barrhead, near Glasgow, to import and market the model.

McKelvie had been a prominent Scottish haulage operator and realised that UK truck-makers of the time were not producing adequate vehicles for the emerging motorways and current regulations. With that in mind, he studied several European truck manufacturers with a view to import a suitable type for the UK market. The Volvo F86 articulated unit was the preferred type, and Ailsa Trucks began importing them in 1967.

Dealerships and agencies were set up as sales of the Volvo F86 quickly showed that UK haulage companies were greatly in favour of the model due to its power, light weight, and superior driver accommodation. It was equally acceptable on local and long-distance haulage at the then UK gross weight of 32 tons.

On the success of the F86, Ailsa Trucks began to import a more powerful Volvo truck, the F88, which had a much larger cab and engine. It became a direct competitor to other high-powered European trucks that were gaining a foothold in the UK market. About this time, ultra-long-distance haulage to the Middle East and beyond was beginning and the F88 was to become a well favoured type for this long-haul work.

As Volvo trucks were taking a sizeable share of the UK market, Ailsa Trucks opened an assembly plant at Irvine in Ayrshire, not many miles away from the original premises in Barrhead. This facility grew to a considerable size and dealt with all Volvo trucks entering the UK market. Bus and coach chassis development took place at Irvine, with the front-engined Ailsa double-deck bus chassis being designed and manufactured there.

Development of Volvo F86 variants took place at Barrhead and subsequently at Irvine, which saw three- and four-axle Volvo trucks being built specifically to suit the needs of the UK market. In later years, the Irvine factory produced large numbers of this type over new model ranges, which found favour in the UK and Irish haulage industry, invoking many repeat orders. Other chassis were developed at Irvine, such as a military 4x4 and various specials, particularly the CH230 for Switzerland, which combined the F10 chassis with an F7 cab.

With the subsequent model upgrades, the Volvo range achieved a high sales rate for trucks over 16 tonnes gross and became a market leader in the UK, thus upholding Jim McKelvie's idea that a superior type of truck was needed in the 1960s UK market. Unfortunately, the UK truck manufacturers did not rise to the challenge of Volvo and the other imported makes, which gradually saw them being eroded away until the point where there are none left today.

Acknowledgements

The majority of the photos used in this book are from my own camera, or from my collection over many years. I would like to thank Pat Crang and Eddie Waugh for the use of their photos, and for their comments on information and photographs passed to me by the late Ken Durston.

The Volvo F86 was the first Volvo model to be imported for sale in the UK. Before that, a similar Volvo truck in LHD form was loaned to a London haulage company for assessment. It was an L4751 type with the cab fitted to the F86. Nothing became of the trial.

When Ailsa Trucks began to import Volvo trucks in 1967, the first type was the F86. The first articulated unit, shown here, was sold to Thomas Hutchinson, who operated in north-east England. It was used on timber and general haulage and has been restored, spending time in the Volvo Museum in Sweden.

Initially, the emphasis was on articulated units, with long wheelbase chassis being available for a gross vehicle weight (GVW) of 16 tons. This type of F86 was heavier and more expensive than the contemporary UK models on offer, although its power output made it suitable as a drawbar unit. This example has seen better days; hopefully it was restored.

The F86 became very popular as an artic unit, being ideal for almost every haulage application. It was equally at home on long-distance haulage and local work. The cab provided a good working environment for the driver. Lester's preserved example looks as if it could go to work at any time.

The basic cab structure on the Volvo F86 did not alter during its production. It was built to Swedish safety regulation, which required it to withstand great forces on impact. Some external modernisation was applied to the front, with a new plastic grille panel. This picture shows how it compared with contemporary DAFs and Scanias. (P. Crang)

As the popularity of the Volvo F86 took off in the UK, other types were developed, firstly as 6x2 rigids, as was the usual setup in Sweden, with a lifting rear axle as seen on this tipper high up in the mountains of Scotland.

VJ Harper is a well-known preservationist of Foden lorries, and to transport them to vintage shows this Volvo F86 was given a complete refurbishment. The clear, all-round visibility is apparent in this view.

The three-axle, or six-wheeler, F86 chassis continued to gain sales and could be specified with different types of rear suspension to suit the intended work. This one is a typical agricultural tipper, with fold-in sides to allow it to be used as a platform lorry.

Long-wheelbase eight-wheelers on the Irvine-developed F86 chassis were exceptionally suitable for bulk haulage or livestock removal, where space was essential on a solid base. The eight-wheel F86 fulfilled that criterion, and this one was thought to be the largest cattle wagon in the south-west of Scotland when it was new.

When developed at Irvine, the eight-wheeler F86 had a newly designed chassis. It was deeper and made the mounting of the cab slightly higher, which fell afoul of UK lighting height arrangements. To get around this the cab was fitted with smaller dual headlamps, which just came under the maximum height rules.

Some Volvo F86 trucks were kept in service for a long time. This one was probably the last still working in southern Scotland. Its longevity was attributed to the driver, Andy McWhirter; when he retired, the Volvo came off the road.

Hayton Coulthard is a long established haulage company and celebrated their centenary in 2016. Duncan Coulthard has this F86 in a small fleet of restored Volvos that are representing the fleet in the past.

The counties of Ayrshire and Lanarkshire were well known for their coalfields. Road haulage was a big factor in the movement of the coal, and this long Volvo F86 was one of the players. It has a massive body in height and length, using a wheelbase more appropriate to a platform lorry. Overloading would be easy!

When the F86 model had become an established and well-liked artic unit, Ailsa Trucks began to import a larger and higher powered model known as the F88. The Volvo F88 had a 240 bhp engine and a higher cab, making it much more suitable for long-distance haulage. It was an instant hit with operators and drivers alike.

Like the F86, the Volvo F88 was available on different chassis configurations and a long-wheelbase drawbar model was on the specification list. It was a well-liked type in Continental haulage, but did not do as well in the UK.

The F88 was designed for a gross combination weight (GCW) of 38 tons, but initially was restricted to 32 tons in the UK. This one is seen with a tri-axle trailer, but would not be able to run at its full potential until 1983, by which time it was probably in disuse.

The peter Haines Volvo F88 is one which was restored to working order. The F88 was such a well thought of truck that many have been restored since the 1990s, and are a common sight at vintage and classic vehicle events.

In 1970, due to changes in power rating per laden weight, Volvo introduced a new 12 litre engine and fitted it in a new truck model designated the F89. The engine was inclined to fit under the F88 cab and it could not be ordered in RHD, which did not suit UK operators. A power upgrade to 290 bhp was introduced for the F88 for the UK, but it was not a universal success.

The F88 was also available as a 6x2 or a 6x4. This one was built as a heavy haulage artic unit with a much higher gross weight rating than a haulage F88.

The F88 continued as Volvo's preferred heavier artic unit and was always seen at the forefront of long distance haulage. It was on sale about the time when the Middle East overland haulage boom began and many UK operators used them on this work.

In the 1990s, the trend for show trucks or classics was becoming evident. The early high-power Volvos were in the vanguard, and this this F88 with metallic paint and graphics was an early example of the 'art'.

The high power rating of the F88 (at the time) led it to being regarded as a good drawbar unit. This one is seen being loaded with livestock, while its trailer is parked elsewhere. It is a three-axle model, well able to support the double-deck livestock container.

The Volvo F88 was held in high esteem, which is notable by their numbers in preservation. This one, a 290 bhp model that is finished in an understated livery, travels throughout the UK to truck shows and road runs.

Another F88 that was restored as a 'classic' truck during the 1990s and 'blinged up' beyond the normal new truck look, was this three-axle unit of T. Streeter. Many modern working trucks are turned out to this standard nowadays.

Further representation of Scottish operators' preferences for high power artic units is this F88 290 bhp in the livery of S. Davidson from Aberdeenshire. Higher power made for shorter journey times in the less-developed road systems of the 1980s. Speed limiters were not required on those days!

The Volvo F89 had a 12 litre 330 bhp engine, which was inclined to the right in the chassis and did not allow RHD controls. It was not ideally suited to UK operators, except for those who did most of their work in Europe and beyond. Geoff Gilbert used several on Middle Eastern haulage.

A version of the Volvo F88 was the G88, which was designed to be used in places where weight regulations required wide spread axles. The G88 had its front axle set further forward, not unlike the typical setup in USA. This example, found in UK fairground service, illustrates the forward-set axle. Some were used as artic units in the UK when GCW was related to axle spread.

In 1977, Volvo embarked on a replacement of the F88 and F89 ranges, with new models that were to be known as the F10 and F12. The models had new, modern cabs and featured developed 10 and 12 litre engines. Both types were available in RHD. Currie European was an early user of the type.

J. A. Alexander used this 1978 Volvo F10 on tipper and low-loader work throughout Scotland. It is seen with a tri-axle trailer that allowed it to run, after 1983, at 38 tons GCW, which its 300 bhp engine was very capable of.

The well-known whisky distillery Johnnie Walker of Kilmarnock used an F10 with a box van trailer at 32 tons GCW. It served the company well, and is seen in its later years with its deep red livery beginning to fade.

Goods vehicle taxation in the 1980s depended on gross weight and axle configurations. The Volvo F10 was designed with a third axle, or pusher, ahead of the driving axle for this reason. The use of a day cab was not common, but would have saved weight and allowed an extra payload, which was often a critical issue in fuel tankers.

Alex Hay has chosen to use a three-axle artic unit with a tri-axle trailer. This would have given a serious reduction on vehicle taxation cost, but would have slightly reduced the payload capacity. There were arguments for and against the taxation rules at the time, which were later relaxed.

Another Scottish fleet well known by its livery and well-kept condition, which now operates mainly Scanias and DAFs, P. & C. Hamilton had this fine F10 on their licence in the 1990s. It has the Globetrotter cab, which allowed greater height and space in the cab when it came onto the market. A non-standard stainless steel bumper has been fitted.

D. Steven & Son is yet another Scottish fleet that is well known for their attractive livery and use of high-power trucks. This F12 is likely to have the 350 bhp 12 litre engine. The horses relate to the beginnings of the company in horse-drawn transport.

A rigid three-axle Volvo F12 which would run with a drawbar trailer on collection and delivery of shipping containers. It has an over-cab sleeper made by Volvo and known as a Eurotrotter. Not a lot of space will have been gained, if any, for a few centimetres of load space.

An F12 in a plain livery but still an eye-catcher. The f12 was well favoured as a powerful unit which could keep to tight journey schedules particularly in the theatrical business in which this one was operated throughout Europe.

1978 saw the introduction of the Volvo F7 range to replace the F86 types which had been instrumental in establishing the Volvo truck marque in the UK. The F7 was equipped with a completely new cab which was a modified version of a cab common the Saviem, DAF, and Magirus Deutz.   (P. Crang)

The Volvo F7 range was made available in a range which covered all the models of the previous F86. This F7, seen in Ayr Harbour, delivering ship's stores, is unusual for an eight-wheeler having a box van body.

The majority of Volvo F7 types were built as artic units on two axles. However, some special orders were filled for twin-steer units, particularly for Shell Oils. The F7 shown here may be one of these units, which is living a second life as a general haulage artic. (K. Durston)

As a four-axle, or eight-wheeler, truck, most F7 types were used as tipper lorries. However, the long-wheelbase model came into its own as a bulk carrier and was taken up by many livestock carriers. They were considered stable enough to carry double or triple livestock bodies.

This Volvo F7 six-wheeler has been equipped to pull a trailer and is seen here with an impressive load of straw bales. Load space is paramount and a day cab creates a little extra platform length, while the cab rack allows four extra Heston bales to be carried. (P. Crang)

A more typical F7 application as an artic unit with a tandem axle tanker trailer can be seen here. Gunnings Motors used this F7 for the carriage of aviation fuel to helicopters working on aerial fertilizer drops.

The Volvo F7 was a very competent tipper chassis and was used in both six- and eight-wheeler forms throughout the UK. This one, rated at 24 tons GVW, has an insulated tarmac body and was operated in the Cumbria and Lancashire areas.

The F7 was seen as a good base for milk tankers and the lifting rear axle, as seen on this one, made for easier manoeuvring in tight farmyards. The Scottish Milk Marketing Board replaced older four-axle tankers with a number of Volvo F7 six-wheelers.

The ability to have a long platform body on a day cab F7 is again seen in this picture. Nichol McKay are steel stockholders and need the body space. The truck is fitted with a lifting rear axle, which when running light would extend the rear overhang, meaning it needed to be watched carefully when undertaking tight turns.

As part of his 'heritage fleet', Duncan Coulthard has also restored a Volvo F7, which is seen here in full Hayton Coulthard livery and a typical Coulthard fleet name.

Alongside the F7 models, Volvo produced a lighter range known as the F6. These had a lower GVW of 16 tons against the F7 design's GVW of 19 tons. The F6 also had a smaller engine, of 180 bhp, and a modified F7 cab. Short and long wheelbase variants were available.

This picture shows an F7 and an F6 side by side and illustrates the difference in the sleeper cab and day cab. Although the cabs appear similar, only the side panels are same. (C. Nicholson)

The sleeper cab was available on the F6 16-tonner, as can be seen on Davie Robinson's platform truck, which is taking part in an Ayrshire road run.

The Volvo F6 was adaptable to various types of bodywork and J. L. Young of Ayr used this one with a large Luton-style van for furniture removals and transport. Pickfords Removals had a large fleet of Volvo F6 vans, and this one may be a former fleet member.

Charlie Street runs a small haulage business in Ayrshire, and one of the mainstays of the fleet was this F6 platform truck. Charlie's fleet was always well kept and finished in the traditional Scottish style.

A 1984 Volvo F6 from the former Macaskill of Stornoway fleet that was – as the wording on the side says – used on distribution in the Highlands of Scotland, and to its island base in the Hebrides, or Western Islands.

Another example of a Volvo F6 used as a removal van with an emphasis on international work. To that end it has a sleeper cab, which might not have given very accommodating living quarters.

This F6 has been built as a straightforward platform truck for the haulage of sawn timber from a Carlisle sawmill. It is seen in the Carlisle Volvo dealership for service or repair, but it has a very well-kept look about it.

The Volvo F6 was also available in short wheelbase form for use as a tipper. This F7 was operated for many years by an owner/driver on contract to a local builder's merchant for bulk deliveries.

The Irvine assembly factory in Scotland had diversified into bus chassis production and was seen by Volvo as being suitable to develop types for smaller markets. In Switzerland the maximum vehicle width was 2.3 metres, and there was a requirement for a minimum of 10 bhp per ton at the 28 tons maximum GVW. The Irvine factory developed the CH230 model using the F7 cab on an F12 chassis in order to conform to the width restriction but achieve the power requirement.

The Volvo F7 was an ideal truck for short- and medium-wheelbase tippers. Although this one looks like a platform truck, the body sides have been folded flat to allow it to carry general cargo, which would have probably been bagged material, either bales of hay or straw. It's a 6x2 with the rear axle lifted.

The low-set cab on the FL models made them ideal as car transporters and this one with eleven cars is a good example of the type contemporary to the 1980s, with a long drawbar unit and an equally sized trailer.

A fine example of a new Volvo FL7 on show at an event before it went to work as a tipper lorry in the east of Scotland around the city of Edinburgh. The low-set cab would be an advantage to a tipper driver, who would be frequently in and out of the cab.

R. Atkinson of Preston had this F10, which was nearly new at the time of the photograph in the then BP Truck stop at Crick. This one is running on six axles in order to take advantage of the lower road tax available. The integrated air management system fits well with the trailer.

Another new Volvo F7, which is still to be fitted with registration plates and fitted out as a domestic fuel tanker for operation in Northern Ireland. The six-wheel FL7 would be able to carry a decent payload of fuel, and would be compact enough to get in and out of tight delivery points.

The FL10 in eight-wheeler guise was, like its predecessors, the F86 and F7 eight-wheelers, a solid base for livestock transport. This one, from the far north of Scotland, has a fairly low livestock body but a third sheep deck could be erected on top.

The six-wheel FL10 on a standard tipper chassis was also a good basis for transit concrete mixers. This one was going to a Northern Ireland concrete manufacturer after it had been displayed on a dealer's stand at a local truck show.

This Volvo FL10 was a 38 ton drawbar unit that was employed on log transport from the forests of Scottish Woodlands. John Twiname from Castle Douglas in southern Scotland was the operator.

James Kingan & Sons Ltd mainly operated this good-looking FL7 drawbar outfit on agricultural haulage and it was often seen with a high load of baled hay or straw, at which its power rating would be no more than adequate.

The FL10 was often specified as an eight-wheel waste disposal truck, as in the application where the engine had to power a hydraulic pump to run the equipment for loading and later tipping or ejection at a landfill site. Another new truck on show at a utility show in Paignton some years ago. (P. Crang)

The FL7 and FL10 in their various wheelbase options allowed for long platform bodies and could be had as a sleeper cab or a day cab. This FL7 has a long livestock body and is seen awaiting a load at Ayr market.

The City of Glasgow Council specified 6x4 FL10 artic units to pull their high-capacity waste trailers. The double-drive rear axles were necessary to get on and off landfill sites.

The fleet of R. & A. Muir is long established as a tipper operator and the majority of the fleet has for a long time been Volvo. This FL7 was to be one of the last of its type in service, and looks particularly well kept considering it was being used in the rough and tumble of tipper work.

An early version of the FL10 in the well-known John Beaty tipper fleet from Penrith in Cumbria can be seen here. The tri-axle tipper trailer indicates it would be running at 38 tons GCW when seen on a wintry day on the old A74 road near Beattock.

McPherson of Aberlour was an independent haulier taken over by the Transport Development Group (TDG), along with many other large hauliers in the UK. This Volvo FL10 had yet to be painted in the rather insipid TDG green, and reminds us of the original company livery.

During the production of the FL10 range, power outputs gradually rose across many manufacturers' ranges. Volvo introduced a premium model with the 12 litre engine, which was to be known as the FL12. This type found favour as an artic unit and as an eight-wheel tipper, where the extra power of the lager engine was beneficial. Outwardly, it looked no different from an FL10.

This FL6 was a 12-tonner and was used as a driver training lorry until new regulations requiring the use of eight-speed gearboxes and a minimum length made it obsolete. The open tipper body type was ruled out at the same time.

Truck Plant Services used this 17 ton GVW FL6 as a carrier for a mobile plant and equipment all around Scotland. It was fitted with a slide-back body in the manner of a recovery truck to ease the loading of wheeled machinery.

Smaller lorries are not a common sight in the UK fairgrounds, but they have their place. This short-wheelbase FL6, which appears to be a former lightweight artic unit, has been rebuilt as a generator and towing van for either light fair rides or a caravan.

A furniture retailer used this smart Luton van on a Volvo FL6 chassis, which was quite long for a 7.5 ton truck, bit volume rather that weight was the criterion.

The FL4 did not sell well as a 7.5 ton non-HGV truck, and in 1997 Volvo developed a lighter version it designated as the FLC. Its sales, however, were only marginally better than the original FL4.

This Volvo FLC was operated on local parcel deliveries by a long-standing company in Ayrshire. The size of the box van was ideal for the purpose and the low cab made the stop-start work easier.

Another variant of the FL range was known as the FS7. This was a combination of the FL6 chassis and cab with the 7 litre engine normally fitted to the FL7 types. The FS7 was seen as a go-between the FL6 and the heavier FL7, but few were sold. This Hydro-Electric FL was fitted out as a drawbar unit, with demountable bodies.

A development of the FL6 was a 4x4 type, which was built as an aircraft tug for the Swedish Airforce. This is an early model, which is seen after being painted in military green.

The FL6 4x4 was offered commercially but not many were built. This one was used by a civil engineer to access off-road sites.

By 1993 Volvo had developed models of high power, high capacity trucks, which were to be known as the FH range. There was to be the FH12, which would be fitted with the 12 litre engine, and the FH16, fitted with the larger 16 litre diesel. There would be no FH10. This Reid's Transport FH12 shows the new cab with the pronounced, aerodynamic slope to the windscreen, which was claimed to reduce internal space.

The well-known Scottish Sam Anderson fleet has latterly been made up largely by Scanias, but several Volvo FH12 units have also been in service over the years. This one, with a curtainside trailer, is set up with six axles in anticipation of forthcoming 44 ton GCW operation.

The FH12 Volvo with double-drive rear axles was a capable heavy haulage unit and this one entered service with Cadzow Heavy Haulage in 2001, rated under Special Types General Orders (STGO) up to 80 tons. It would not be working hard on the day of the photograph!

Scotlee Transport runs a mixed fleet and had a number of Volvo FH12 units on international refrigerated haulage. The Scotlee livery of blue, red and white makes a great advert for the firm.

The FH12 was also available with a tag-axle behind the driving axle. T. Anderson & Son are agricultural and forestry equipment engineers and used this FH12 to transport machinery for repair and maintenance. The lifting tag-axle would help when manoeuvring the long low-loader trailer.

The early Volvo FH12 models are making an appearance in the fairgrounds – once the preserve of ERFs and Fodens. This one, a 6x4 model, possibly a former heavy haulage artic, has been rebuilt as a generator and heavy tractor. It is seen attached to a long trailer with a dolly drawbar and must be an impressive sight on the road.

The Horne family use this FH12 to pull one of their large rides on a semi-trailer engineered to be part of the attraction. The trailer has steerable rear axles and the whole outfit is in immaculate condition.

Tanker operation was feasible with a bonneted unit as tanker trailers tended to be shorter. This UK-registered NH12 is pulling a trailer from its European company. It has been fitted with a small-wheeled pusher axle to accommodate 44 tons GCW.

When truck racing came into vogue in the UK, most of the racers were hastily modified road-going trucks. As truck racing developed, more modified racers began to appear, and this N series Volvo is an example, but is quite unsophisticated compared to modern-day racers.

Over the years, Volvo produced some modified trucks to suit particular types of work. Loanhead Transport, an associated company of the larger W. H. Malcolm business, had high ground clearance tippers, due to straight front axles and modified suspension. The higher chassis caused the headlamps to be relocated in the bumper.

Terberg is a Dutch company that makes specialist trucks based on Volvo components. JST Services of Ayr had this Terberg 2000, ground pressure, eight-wheel-drive truck and trailer to haul timber out of forests to loading areas for road-going trucks. It has all the appearance of a Volvo FM.

Tom French & Son have been long-term Volvo users and this FH12 is typical of a largely identical fleet running at 44 tons GCW.

McGawn Bros, of Maybole in Ayrshire, are well known for their truck show award winning older Scanias. This Volvo FH12 was added to the fleet and given a basic rendition of the usual green and red livery.

W. H. Malcolm is the larger fleet operator in Scotland, with a high proportion of Volvos in the fleet. This FM represents a curtain-sided truck in the Logistics fleet, running in a modern version of the traditional fleet livery.

The Irish truck market has been good for Volvo, with many Volvo trucks having been operated on both sides of the border. Clearway is a scrap metal business from Portadown, in Northern Ireland, and their FH was hauling scrap to a yard in Belfast docks.

Although seen here in Chivas Regal Whisky livery, this FH is a contract tanker from the fleet of McPherson of Aberlour (formerly part of the Transport Development Group).

The Volvo FH and FM artic units have become the majority in the Northern Ireland-based McBurney Transport fleet. This FM is seen on the southern end of the A77, cruising through the rolling Ayrshire landscape.

J. B. Rawcliffe & Sons is a well-known heavy haulage company with a large number of Volvos in their fleet. This smart FH has an extendable trailer and was taking a break in a service area on the M74.

The FM models continued as before. The FM10 was often found in eight-wheeler configuration as a farmyard bulk feed-tipper, and Carrs Billington operated this one from their Carlisle depot.

In 2012 Volvo introduced a new range of FH types, which included the FH13 and the FH16. The new cabs had a similarity to the previous FH cabs but were completely new, sharing a structure that was later to be seen on heavy Renault trucks. The new cab is seen to its advantage in this example, which is operated at 44 tons GCW by Iain Watt & Son.

Ferguson Transport of Fort William and Invergordon are Volvo service dealers, and their fleet is made up in the majority by Volvo Trucks. This FH was travelling through Onich on the road to Glasgow from Fort William.

Northern Ireland haulage operators were not slow to take up the new FH. This Surefreight curtain-sided artic shows off the more vertical windscreen on the new cab, which was said to allow more internal space while retaining good aerodynamic characteristics

Harry Lawson, from Broughty Ferry, near Dundee, is a long-established haulier who ran a UK-manufactured fleet until no more were available. The company tried several European types and eventually settled on Volvos. This fine example, which is in traditional style, was seen taking a break on its journey south one Sunday afternoon in 2017.

A Volvo FH16 with the most powerful 16 litre engine, at 750 bhp, running back from a wind farm load movement in southern Scotland. Axle weight requirements have seen a rise in numbers of 8x4 units up to and beyond 150 tons GCW.

Capable of 750 bhp, this FH16 will be well able to cope with recovery work. Without a doubt, this is a stunning vehicle for UK and European recovery.

Meanwhile, the FH13 goes from strength to strength. This Ferguson Transport FH appears to be quite new at the time of the photograph. It is running light, with the tag-axle lifted.

Three new FH13 units for Scottish hauliers lined up on the Volvo stand at the 2016 Scottish Truckfest.

Another new FH13 standing in the yard of JST Services awaiting registration, after which it will be put into service on log haulage.

The more southern parts of the A77 trunk road through Ayrshire are quite narrow and are used by many heavy trucks every day. There is no time for complacency, as seen here with the Neil Cluckie FH, which is passing a similar-sized Mulgrew artic.

The Volvo factory at Irvine was able to design and build one-off specials. Irvine produced this long 8x6 for naval research into torpedoes. The front axle was driven and there was a winch under the body. It eventually made its way into fairground service with a member of the Danter family.

The N10/12 was never built at Irvine, but several were imported as heavy haulage tractors. This one, built as a heavy locomotive, to use its legal title, tours the country as a 'showman's special', with the massive trailer on tow, plus one other trailer, which, in this instance, is a small kiosk.